MW00395496

This book belongs to:

____